OUT OF THE WILDERNESS:
ONE STEP AT A TIME

Twelve Months of an Inspirational Journey

SHERRY NORTON

WESTBOW
PRESS®
A DIVISION OF THOMAS NELSON
& ZONDERVAN

WestBow Press books may be ordered through booksellers or by contacting:

WestBow Press
A Division of Thomas Nelson & Zondervan
1663 Liberty Drive
Bloomington, IN 47403
www.westbowpress.com
1 (866) 928-1240

ISBN: 978-1-9736-0800-4 (sc)
ISBN: 978-1-9736-0799-1 (e)

Library of Congress Control Number: 2017917667

Print information available on the last page.

WestBow Press rev. date: 12/04/2017

CONTENTS

WAYS DIRECTED

WHO IS HE?

WHERE ARE WE GOING?

HE IS

AUTHOR'S NOTE

This book is more than a devotional. It is a combination an inspirational devotional *and* journal. There are places to journal throughout the text, and there are also extra pages if more journaling as desired. All scriptures are found in the King James Version of the Bible. I hope that my thoughts and poems will also encourage and bless you.

SHARED THOUGHTS

Month 1, Week 1

Being blind physically is nothing like being spiritually blind. I should know because I have experienced both. Now that I know there's a difference, I would rather remain physically blind than go back to the spiritual blindness that was my life for years. In my spiritual blindness, I was really in the dark—full of fear and filled with hopelessness. In physical blindness, there is still light in a darkened room, and the colors are beautiful to behold because I know and am secure in the fact that God Almighty is with me. I did not have that reassurance while I was spiritually blind. This doesn't mean there aren't times when I'm a little shaky and hesitant to take the next step. But I look to God as my source and my strength, as well as my protection, and I remind myself of God's promises so that I will take a step closer to Him, even if it's a small one.

Don't Feel Sorry For Me
My eyes may miss more of what you see,
But please don't feel sorry for me.
I may not see your lovely face or tell the color of your hair,
But God has blessed me with color and light
I wish that I could share.

Even in the darkest rooms, it is not dark to me,
for God has given me color and light beautiful to see.
So please do not feel sorry for me.
I would God's beauty you would see.

My eye may miss some beauty here on earth,
But God's glorious light, I count much more worth. Amen.

Day 1: Exodus 24:17

Day 2: Deuteronomy 28:34

Day 3: Ecclesiastes 6:9

Day 4: Ecclesiastes 11:7–9

Day 5: Isaiah 5:15, 19–21

Day 6: Isaiah 11:2–3

Day 7: 2 Corinthians 5:7

Month 1, Week 2

I still wonder at the fact that God loves me, and He loves you too. Even if I were the only person on earth, He still would have sent His Son, Jesus Christ, my Lord and Savior, to die on that cross and be the bridge that brought His Father, God, and man back in the place of fellowship that we have belonged in from the very beginning. God is so merciful and loves us, though He hates our sin. He is a holy God and has no part of sin, making a way for us to be cleansed from sin and snatched away from the very gates of hell, where we would spend eternity being separated from God and life eternal in Him. We were choosing to walk in the dark and, in pleasing ourselves, were spiritually blind.

God's Love
April 2001

God's love sent His Son to earth.
God's love made the way.
God's love kept Him upon that cross,
Until the penalty for us He did pay.

God's love put Him in that tomb.
God's love brought Him forth again.
And God's love gave us another chance to come close to Him.

God's love brought us from death to life.
God's love brought us out of darkness and into the marvelous light.
God's love brought us back to Him
Through His only begotten Son, Jesus Christ.

There is no love without God's love.
There is no love without Him,
There is no love without God's love.
Open your heart and welcome Him in. Amen.

Day 8: Deuteronomy 23:4–5

Day 9: 1 Corinthians 2:9–10

Day 10: John 3:16

Day 11: John 16:27

Day 12: Ephesians 2:4

Day 13: 2 Thessalonians 2:16–17

Day 14: 1 John 4:7–12

Month 1, Week 3

Think of it. God the Father loves us very much, and His thoughts toward us are good. Open your eyes and look around you. It doesn't look like God even cares. Well, that's part of the problem. You can't go by the things that natural eyes see. That is what the enemy of God wants you to do. God has already proved His love, when He gave us His only begotten Son, our Savior, Jesus Christ, who came down to this earth, taking on flesh and dwelling among us. To go back even farther, from the very beginning, God gave man the right to choose right from wrong, light from dark, good from evil, life from death, blessing from cursing, and love from hate. With my right to choose, I have chosen to be my Father God's child, and I follow after Him.

Dearest Child
July 2001

Dearest child close to My heart,
I love You
But not what keeps us apart.
I draw You and wooed You and call You My own.
But how much am I really known?

You ask and seek and knock at the door,
But all You want is more, more, more.
You would be amazed of My plans for You.
Come and seek My face and try something new.
To You, My child, for whom much abounds,
Who once was lost but now is found.
Dearest child, the apple of My eye,
Knowest that I am always nearby.
Love, Your heavenly Father. Amen.

Day 15: Deuteronomy 30:15–19

Day 16: Proverbs 1:29–33

Day 17: Proverbs 3:31

Day 18: Joshua 24:15

Day 19: Philippians 1:22–24

Day 20: Nehemiah 9:7

Day 21: Isaiah 14:1

Month 1, Week 4

Have you ever been tired of going over the same ground again and again? Tired of taking two steps forward just to be pulled three steps back because your past has not let you go? Or have you shaken it off, speaking the popular words "if only"? Living in our past does not get us into our present, and we can forget our future under those circumstances. Well, I got very tired of that happening. As a matter of fact, I got angry about it and was quite determined to get past myself, getting out of my comfort zone of self-pity and fear. Yes, you read it right: I wrote "fear," the fear of missing God's perfect will, the fear of failing, the fear of allowing someone to deceive me again and again.

Crossing Over This Jordan
June 2002

I am determined. I have purposed in my heart
that I am crossing over this Jordan that I am facing.
I am looking to my God up above,
who has said that He will never leave me or forsake me.
I can do all things through Christ, who strengthens me.
For only in Him am I able.;
For only in Him am I set free.
For he whom the Son sets free is free indeed.
Arise and go stepping away from what has been holding you back,
for fear is a terrible thing.
Say goodbye to all your hurts;
press always ahead, one step at a time.
And when you give them to God, whatever you do, don't take them back.
For the devil is a liar out to kill, steal, and destroy.
He doesn't want you to know the fullness of God's joy.
He wants to keep you wrapped up in his evil plans and ploys.
I am taking hold of Jesus's hand;
I am following by His side.
I am pressing on toward the mark with God as my guide.
I am determined, and I have purpose in my heart.
I Am crossing over this Jordan that is facing me.
I am looking to my God up above,
and He will never leave me or forsake me.
I can do all things through Christ who strengthens me.
For only in Him am I able.
For only in Him am I set free.
For he whom the Son sets free is free indeed.

Arise and go stepping away from what has been holding you back,
for fear is a terrible thing.
Say goodbye to all your hurts;
press always ahead, one step at a time.
When you give them to God, whatever you do, don't take them back.
For the devil is a liar out to kill, steal, and destroy.
He doesn't want you to know the fullness of God's joy.
He wants to keep you wrapped up in his evil plans and ploys.
I am determined, and I have purpose in my heart
that I am crossing over this Jordan that is facing me.
I am looking to my God up above,
and He will never leave me or forsake me.
I can do all things through Christ who strengthens me.
For only in Him am I able.
For only in Him am I set free.
For he whom the Son sets free is free indeed.
I am taking hold of Jesus's hand;
I am following by His side.
I am pressing on toward the mark with God as my guide. Amen.

Day 22: Deuteronomy 4:31–32

Day 23: Philippians 3:13–16

Day 24: Exodus 14:13

Day 25: Exodus 15:16

Day 26: Genesis 15:1

Day 27: Deuteronomy 20:1, 3, 5–8

Day 28: Deuteronomy 31:6, 8

Month 1, Week 5

Stepping out into the unknown can be a terrifying thing, but if we have our eyes constantly on the One who gives us strength, equips us in powering us to step out of the boat on top of those stormy seas, then He will not let us be overthrown. As a child of God, we have reassurance that we are in the palm of His hand, and nothing and no one can snatch us out of that mighty hand. Doing it on our own will fail, but by doing it in the power and the might of our Lord and Savior, Jesus Christ, we will succeed. He keeps us, upholds us, equips us, and strengthens us for all that He has us do. We are not here on this earth for ourselves. We are here as His ambassadors to do of His good and perfect will. Be like Peter in stepping out of the boat, but do not be like Peter and take your eyes off God.

Walk with Me
October 2000

Walk with me hand in hand
and face-to-face.
Walk with me, O Lord; great is Your grace.
I'm in You, and You're in me.
I in You will stand victoriously.
O, my Lord, great is Your grace.

Walk with me through day and night.
Walk with me, my hope of hopes and light of lights.
Walk with me, O Lord; great is Your grace, my life's delight.
I'm in You, and You are in me.
I in You will stand victoriously,
O, my Lord, great is Your grace.

Walk with me till eternity reigns.
Walk with me heart-to-heart
and name to name.
Walk with me, O Lord. You are forever the same.
I'm in You, and You are in me,
I in You will stand victoriously,
O, my Lord, great is Your grace. Amen.

Day 29: Isaiah 17:7–8

Day 30: Hebrews 12:2

Day 31: Jude 1:21

Month 2, Week 1

What is commitment to God? Being committed to our first love, Jesus Christ, even though this world tries to draw us away with its glitter and glitz and good pleasure that does not last for very long, we do not see the traps, the snares, or the pits laid out along that way. Is it worth it when we betray our Lord, when we have our own way? My answer is *no*, for the tradeoff is too great to pay of days, weeks, months or years of pleasure for an eternity without Him. For me, again, I say *no*!

One's Commitment
April 2000

What does it mean to commit—
to make a commitment?
Does it mean being there only when things are going well?
When we are benefited and blessed
and things are going our way?
When we don't have to struggle,
even through hard places, or suffer a little bit maybe?
When we don't have to put anything out of ourselves,
and are always looking to receive?
When our focus is on the self being taken care of
and is at our ease?
No. That to me would be a lonely, lonely world.
Without the love, grace,
and selfless act of our heavenly Father and Lord,
we would not be here.
Where all have sinned and fallen short of the glory of God.
Though He knew that He would have to descend from heaven,
away from His heavenly Father,
and be born as a man-child on this earth.
Though He knew that He would have to suffer persecution,
verbal and physical abuse, and rejection.
Though He was homeless, lied on, betrayed,
and put on trial.
Though all He did was commit to doing His Father's will,
and becoming hope of eternal life to all those who believe on Him.
He took all of our sins, iniquity, and blemishes upon Himself.
He was scourged, spit upon, mocked, and nailed to a tree,
and He died a guilty man's death who was not guilty for you and me.
But behold: on the third day after being placed in a tomb,
He rose again victoriously.

So rejoice! Our promise is sure of everlasting life,
with our heavenly Father through His Son.
The results of Jesus's commitment to love, honor, and obey His Father,
Gaining the victory over sin, death, hell, and the grave,
waits for that day of His second coming.
When He will come gather all those who have committed their lives unto Him,
and His Father. Amen.

Day 1: Jeremiah 8:12

Day 2: Ezekiel 6:8–14

Day 3: Ezekiel 18:21–24

Day 4: 1 Samuel 24:16–19

Day 5: Revelation 21:3–8

Day 6: Matthew 25:35–46

Day 7: Leviticus 18:1–30

Month 2, Week 2

What are we going to do when we have to stand before God Almighty and answer for all that we have done—for the words we have spoken and for the things we didn't do? I don't have the answer for that question, even for myself, except to fall on the mercies of God and change my ways while I am still down here on this earth. I can do it with God's help, before it's too late. I will also make sure that I am clear with God up to now by asking forgiveness, but not without trying to change. I'll ask for help to change because I have found out the hard way I cannot change myself. No matter how much I want to, no matter how strong I think I am, no matter how powerful I think my will is, it is not good enough, and on my own it never will be.

Would You Do That if Jesus Were Standing By?
October 2000

Take a stool;
Bend an elbow.
That won't matter.
Who cares? No one you know comes here anyway.
Did you give your life to Jesus Christ?
Would you do that if He were standing by?
Speaking things that belong in the trash
or down in the gutter with the sewage?
Is that how Jesus spoke?
Would you do that if Jesus were standing by?
Push, shove, and kick till they bleed,
because they don't live like you and me?
Is that what Jesus taught
when He walked upon this earth?
Would you do that if Jesus were standing by?
Well, guess what? He is!
So please, before you do,
think, or speak, ask this question of yourself:
Would I do this if Jesus Christ were standing by?
If not, don't. Amen.

Day 8: Psalm 1:1–6

Day 9: Psalm 9:1–10

Day 10: Psalm 37:1–40

Day 11: Psalm 37:1–40

Day 12: Ecclesiastes 11:1–10

Day 13: 2 Corinthians 5

Day 14: 2 Corinthians 5:1–21

Month 2, Week 3

Can you imagine standing before God and knowing you have done all these marvelous works for God, only to hear, "Depart from Me, ye worker of iniquity; I never knew you." To me, those words would be horribly devastating. By choosing God's way and not our own way, or the god of this world's way, the devil, we should hear instead, "Ye have done well. Enter in thy good and faithful servant." Those are words I strive to hear. How about you? In the Bible, we also find these words: "I would that you be hot or cold, but not lukewarm, for if you are lukewarm, I will vomit you out of My mouth." Trying to have the best of both worlds does not work. Straddling the fence causes God to vomit us out of His mouth.

The Road
September 1999

This road I am on, it leads to two.
Which one will you follow?
The one called truth or the other lies?
Which one can you swallow?

This road I am on, it leads to two.
Which one can you see?
The one called light or the other dark?
Which will set you free?

This road I am on, it leads to two.
Which one can you walk?
The one called narrow, or the other wide?
Which one leads to the rock? Amen.

Day 15: Revelation 1, 2, 3

Day 16: Ezekiel 36:16–38

Day 17: Romans 3:1–31

Day 18: 1 Corinthians 11:31–32

Day 19: James 2:12–13

Day 20: 1 Peter 4:1–19

Day 21: Revelation 11:1–19

Month 2, Week 4

"Open the eyes of my heart, Lord. Open the eyes of my heart." Those are beautiful words, and they are also a song. Every time I hear that song, I think to myself, "Yes, amen." The words after that say, "For I want to see you." After hearing those words, my heart's cry is, "Let me see others as You see them, Father. And let them see the You that is in me. Let Your glory show through me." Have you ever felt that way? I think that I am not alone, but there are others who try to stay in their own little worlds, and they do not allow others to touch their lives. I understand these people: for once you have been wounded by someone or several people. You tend to want to close in on yourself, but that will not work because they have forgotten that we are our own worst enemies. Until we take the chance and open ourselves up to loving others as God loves others, we have not lived, even if it means getting hurt in the process. Haven't we hurt God at one time or another? Are we better than Him?

If We Only Knew
June 2001

O, my God, if we only knew the affects for good
or evil that come from our words and deeds.
O God, change us, I plea.
Every time I put my arms around my fellow man with a Godly hug,
I am hugging a part of You, my God.
Every time I speak good
or evil of my fellow man,
I am speaking of You, my God.
Every time I am doing something
or not, I am doing it
or not unto You, O God.
Every time I go the extra mile or not,
I am going that extra mile
or not for You, my God.
Open our eyes, ears, and hearts, and reveal to us Your truths.
Open our eyes, ears, and hearts, my God, and make us more like You.
O, my God, if we only knew the affects for good
or evil that comes from our words and deeds,
what a difference there would be. Amen.

Day 22: Deuteronomy 6:20–25

Day 23: Deuteronomy 10:17–22

Day 24: Deuteronomy 11:1–7

Day 25: Deuteronomy 29:1–29

Day 26: Joshua 24:1–33

Day 27: 1 Samuel 5:1–12; 1 Samuel 6:1–21

Day 28: 1 Samuel 12:1–25

Month 2, Week 5: For the Leap Year

"Lord, there are so many out there who are hurting and lost—far too many for me to help. So what do you, God, want me to do about it? I am only one person!" Have you ever felt that way, or better yet, have you said something like it? Well, doing nothing is definitely not the answer. You may be only one person, but if many of those who can step up are willing to do something, the task will not look so daunting or impossible. For example, a kind word, a warm smile, a Godly hug, praying with or for someone, a card, a poem, paying a bill, buying some food, making something for someone—the list can go on. Let others know that you think enough of them to take time on their behalf. Let them know that they are special to you and especially to God.

God, Here Am I
December 2003

I am only one person,
but God, here am I.
Use me as You see fit.
I am only one person.
So, God, what can I do?
Help me find the right thing to do.
Here are my hands.
what can I make?
Here are my feet.
Where can I go?
Here is my mouth.
What can I say?
Here is my heart.
Who receives Your love?
Please let me know.
I am only one person,
but God, use me as You see fit.
I am only one person.
What, I pray, can I do this day? Amen.

For Every Leap Year:
Day 29: Mark 9:35–42

Month 3, Week 1

What if they laugh at me? What if they reject what God has me say to them? What if he makes fun of me? What if she curses me out? What if they talk about me, and it's all lies? So what! The God that is in you is bigger than them. "If God is for me, who can be against me?" Do it anyway. Whom should we please? Who made us? Whom do we follow? Whom do we answer to in the end? If God cannot use you, He will raise up someone who is willing to do it, Your treasure will not be built up in heaven, but down here on this earth, which will burn up in the end. God's love is sufficient in taking us through any situation, as long as we turn to Him, our Creator.

Sufficient Grace
March 2000

Out of the darkness came the light;
in the beginning was the word.

There is no loss in abundance;
in Christ Jesus, all our needs are met.

Out of despair, gave ye hope.
Unto us a child is born;
unto us a son is given.
Putting down hatred and showing love,
For which God said,
"My grace is sufficient."

Deny foolishness and obtain wisdom,
for thine is the wisdom, and
the power and the glory, forever.

Wipe out ignorance with a flood of knowledge.
Show me thy ways, O Lord.
Teach me thy ways to go.

Forsake war and embrace peace.
And if I be lifted up,
I will draw all men unto me. Amen.

Day 1: Psalm 56:1–13

Day 2: Isaiah 45:1–25

Day 3: Jeremiah 32:21–30

Day 4: Hosea 13:1–16

Day 5: Mark 10:1–16

Day 6: Luke 18:1–17

Day 7: Romans 12:1–21

Month 3, Week 2

Have you ever stopped to hear the cries? Hear them; they are full of hopelessness, despair, and pain. God hears them all the time, and He uses people like you and me to answer those cries. God uses the foolish to confound the wise, and He uses the weak to confound the strong. Let Him use you.

Do You Hear the Cries?
April 2000

Are you hearing their cries for help?
Listen: you can hear their pain and despair.
The fields are ripe for harvest,
but the laborers are few.
"How many more will die without me?" sayeth the Lord.

Come, bring them as my sheep.
You are blessed who have come to me
and have been adopted into the royal family.
But there are way too many who have not.
Unless you come and do your part,
you'll keep hearing the cry of their hearts.

"Help me—I'm falling.
There is no hope.
Help me; I am afraid.

Is anyone there?
Does anyone care?"
Who will go?
Who will say, "Send me, Lord. Send me"? Amen.

Day 8: Isaiah 6:1–8

Day 9: Matthew 15

Day 10: John 13:1–20

Day 11: John 20:1–23

Day 12: Acts 22:1–21

Day 13: Luke 10:1–42

Day 14: Romans 12:10, 13–21

Month 3, Week 3

Doing unto others as you would have done to you is not just a quaint saying—those are words to live by. If you do not want to be treated the way you are treating someone else, then stop it! Other people are made in the image of God just as you are. Whether or not they have chosen to submit themselves under the mighty hand of God yet is between them and God, not you. If all of us were really treated the way we deserved, we all would be going to hell, because none of us are good enough by ourselves. For this reason, God the Father sent God the Son, our Lord and Savior Jesus Christ, down here to earth to pay the price for sin for us by taking our place. Let's not let this great gift of love go to waste. Practice treating others as you would like to be treated, whether or not you feel they deserve to be. Do not be among the goats.

My Precious Gift
August 2000

These are the lies that bombard us all throughout our lives.
You are unwanted, an accident,
a mistake; you are ugly, you are dumb.
You are stupid, you are lazy, you are good for nothing, you will never do anything right.
You won't amount to anything, you are a failure, and no one can love you.
Thank God that these are all lies.
There are probably more that have not been mentioned,
but just throw them in with the rest.
Let's tear down that which destroys, defeats, and is critical,
for this is not of God.

All that God is: healing, renewing,
rebuilding, cleaning up, loving, strengthening,
empowering. He's our hope, our resting place,
the peace that passes all understanding,
and so much more that is good.

I thank God for His only begotten Son
whom He gave, and I thank God
for His Son who gave His life.
God's love had been my precious gift.

During the stormy seas,
He's a solid foundation on which to stand.
Let God's love take away all the hurt,
a lifeline in the pain, sorrow, bitterness,
the anger, tears, and hopelessness.
Instead, let God fill you with love, peace, joy, long suffering,
goodness, gentleness, temperance, and faith.

When we make God our everything
and say that we can do nothing of ourselves,
then we can rejoice and truly say
of a truth: God's love is my precious gift. Amen.

Day 15: John 13:34–35

Day 16: Romans 12:9–10, 14–15

Day 17: Romans 13:7–10

Day 18: Galatians 5:6, 13–18, 22–23

Day 19: Ephesians 4:2–3, 15–16

Day 20: 1 Thessalonians 3:6, 12

Day 21: 1 John 4:7–12, 16–21

Month 3, Week 4

Have you ever noticed that when you point a finger at someone or something, there are three pointing back at you? There is a good scripture in the Bible that goes something like this: Before you try taking the speck out of someone else's eye, get the plank out of your own eye. We as humans are born in iniquity, and we have a tendency in tearing apart another person to make ourselves look or feel good. When the shoe is on the other foot, we do not like it. Let me ask you something: Do you think that other person liked being torn down? We should be wise as a serpent but gentle as a dove. Jesus went as a lamb before the slaughter and opened not His mouth. He is our example, and He was not weak in the way He acted. It took strength to be able to do that. It is all in the way we see things and then put them into practice. Let's try practicing love, mercy, forgiveness, and compassion instead of hatred, vengeance, unforgiveness, and hardness.

A Work in Progress
August 2002

Like a piece of clay upon the potter's wheel,
being shaped and molded, I am learning to be still.
Sitting on the artist's easel,
partly taking shape, I rest in what His finished picture will make.
Just like a building with a solid foundation,
the walls go up strong and built to last.
Then overhead, the rafters and beams.
Overlaid is the roof very tightly seemed.
Next come the doors and windows and seals,
fitted tight against evils ills.
Being far from finished,
what the builder starts, He is surely able to complete,
if we will it in our hearts. Amen.

Day 22: Lamentations 2:31–36

Day 23: Deuteronomy 17:8–13

Day 24: Matthew 7:1–5, 12, 15–20

Day 25: Luke 6:31, 37–38

Day 26: John 7:16–24, 51

Day 27: Romans 14:3–6, 10, 12–16, 18–23

Day 28: James 2:1–13

Month 3, Week 5

Each time we reject human beings or talk about them behind their backs, we are doing it to God, who made us in His own image. Can we honestly withhold our love and still call ourselves followers of Christ? What happens when we refuse to forgive? Why are we bound in that place? We cannot earn the love of God, but we simply walk in His grace. For we are not here for pleasure of the self, but for others who need to be shown the way through our actions. God is guiding us every step of the way, if we let Him. God will not force us after giving us the freedom to choose, and so He sits back and watches us treat some like enemies and others like friends, whether to their faces or behind their backs. All the time, we are forgetting that all are made in the image and likeness of God, created by Him, and if they had been the only ones to be here when Jesus died on the cross, He would have died for them as well as for you or me. We are not doing it unto man but unto our God Most High.

Our God Most High
August 2001

Taste and see how good God is.
Look and see His awesomeness.
Bow before Almighty God,
Who made all the heavens and the earth.

Rejoice and praise His holy name,
soaring to the sky a song of praise
with a thank-filled heart lifting God Almighty high.

Seek God's face and not His hands.
Choose God's holy way and not man's.
Rest in God's abiding arms
and find hope, peace, love, and strength.

Rejoice and praise His holy name,
soaring to the sky a song of praise
from a thank-filled heart lifting God Almighty high.

Trust that God means good for you.
Keep yourself in all His ways.
Walk in God's holy word every single day.

Rejoice and praise His holy name,
soaring to the sky a song of praise
with a thank-filled heart lifting up Almighty God high.

Rejoice and praise His holy name,
soaring to the sky a song of praise
with a thank-filled heart lifting up El' El' Yone,
our God Most High. Amen.

Day 29: Matthew 25:31–45

Day 30: Hebrews 6:4–15

Day 31: 1 John 3:1–24

Month 4, Week 1

Be ye reassured, fear not, and know that God is always with those who have accepted Jesus Christ as their Lord and Savior, for He promised that He would never leave us or for sake us, and He is not a man so that He should lie. Did He not say it? Then it is so. He who has started a good work in you is able to complete it. These words are found in one book among other words that can instruct us, guide us, encourage us, caution us, free us, and reveal unto us our Creator, Savior, best friend, and Lord. This book is called The Holy Bible, and it is the Word of Almighty God.

The Book
November 1999

There is a book I like to read
whose words dwell in my heart.
There is a book I like to read,
whose words set me apart.

There is a book that
tells me of a pure and simple love.
There is a book that
tells me of a heaven up above.

There is a book that
shows me who has made this earth.
There is a book that
shows me how much more I am worth.

There is a book that
leads me from darkness into light.
There is a book that
leads me from death into life.

There is a book that
keeps me on this narrow way.
There is a book that
keeps me from sinning day by day.

This book that I have spoken of, I hope you find it too.
God's peace and love for all mankind,
His Son has already proved. Amen.

Day 1: 2 Timothy 3:7–9, 14–17

Day 2: Psalm 18:21–24, 30–36

Day 3: Psalm 68:1–3, 18–21

Day 4: Psalm 119

Day 5: Proverbs 13:13–20

Day 6: Isaiah 8:10–11, 16

Day 7: Isaiah 40:8, 27–31

Month 4, Week 2

Instead of "One day at a time, sweet Jesus," which are words to a song, I say, "One step at a time, sweet Jesus." I know that my steps are ordered by the Lord. "Man might plan his way, but God directs his steps." The steps of a righteous man are ordered by God. I hold to these words, which are found in God's holy Word, because without His guidance, I would be lost. Truly I'd be a blind person without hope, purpose, or direction, and I'd be filled with confusion. No, thank you. I've done that and been there, and I do not want it again.

Every Step I Take
June 2003

Every step I take,
You are with me all the way.
You lead me, guide me,
Direct my steps, and carry me when I can't.
Every step I take,
You are with me all the way.
I tried to do it without You, God,
but oh, what a mess I made.
Every step I take,
You are with me all the way.
For I now choose God,
to follow You and pray to never stray.
Amen.

Day 8: Psalm 37:23–26, 28, 31, 33–34, 39–40

Day 9: Exodus 13:3, 9–10, 21–22

Day 10: Numbers 14:11–35

Day 11: Nehemiah 9:6–38

Day 12: Luke 1:68–79

Day 13: Isaiah 58:2–14

Day 14: Proverbs 16:2–9, 11, 20, 33

Month 4, Week 3

I was sitting in a college classroom, being instructed in my second semester of English, and wondering whether I was in the wrong classroom. In high school, despite the lack of maturity level there, I tried to learn. Finally around the last week of that semester, I was prompted to write and share the next two items shared here—a letter and a poem.

Dear Fellow Traveler,

My heart cries. Time is not waiting for us to choose to grow up or to find our way. The possibilities are endless, but what a waste if we choose to blindly go on our way in the name of freedom of self-expression. When we are older and have children who are not mature enough to make the choices that they are making but think they are, will we look back and remember those days when we were in the same position. Maturity does not mean you're old enough to go to college, and neither does it mean that a person is old enough to vote or drive. Maturity means taking responsibility for one's actions, respecting other fellow travelers on this road called life, and realizing that the choices made now will affect the future.

Love,
A fellow traveler, Sherry Norton

Choices
September 1999

There are choices in our lives every day we live.
Make these choices for the right, and see what God shall give:
Light instead of darkness on this path we walk.
Love instead of hatred for our fellow man.
Wisdom instead of foolishness to build our house upon the Rock.
And knowledge instead of ignorance for all God's plan for man.
There are choices in our lives every day we live.
Make these choices for the right, and see what God shall give.
As for me, I choose the Lord. Amen.

Day 15: 2 Peter 1:3–9

Day 16: 1 Peter 2:1–17

Day 17: Psalm 74:20–23

Day 18: 1 Peter 3:1–12

Day 19: Romans 12:1–10

Day 20: Proverbs 14:2–3, 6–8, 18, 23, 25

Day 21: Proverbs 15:2, 4, 7, 14, 23, 26, 28, 30–33

HOPE OUT OF THE PAINFUL PLACES

Month 4, Week 4

Through the love of my heavenly Father and the work that He has done and is still doing, my prayer is to turn that which was meant for evil to good. There is hope, and you are not alone. I hope this page and all these pages will encourage, bless, and embolden you to take the step that will bring you out from behind the mask and say, "Devil, you are a liar, and the truth is not in you. In Jesus Christ's name, you are defeated. The power of the past I let you beat me over the head with is broken. No more! Father God, let the victory over my past help others." In Jesus's name. Amen.

Hope Still
April 2000

Whatever your hand finds to do, do it with all your might.
The race is not to the swift,
nor the battle to the strong,
nor bread to the wise,
nor riches to men of understanding,
nor favor to men of skill.
For time and chance happen to them all,
and man also does not know his time,
like fish caught in a cruel net,
like birds caught in a snare.
The sons of men are snared in an evil time
when it falls suddenly upon them.
So that which you must do, do quickly.
Ask, and it shall be given;
seek, and you shall find;
knock, and the door shall be opened unto you.
I am the truth, the way, and the life,
No man cometh unto the Father,
lest he come through me.

"I am the door; come,
enter in," sayeth the Lord my God,
"Come. He who asks shall be given,
he who seeks shall find,
he who knocks the door shall be open unto him." Amen.

Day 22: Deuteronomy 4:31–35

Day 23: Job 13:15–16

Day 24: Job 14:5–9

Day 25: Psalm 16:1–11

Day 26: Psalm 31:1–24

Day 27: Psalm 33:12–22

Day 28: Psalm 42:1–11

Month 4, Week 5

This next piece was written in May 2002 in response to a class I had attended about marriage and having no regrets. I'm celebrating twenty-six years of marriage on October 26. I give God thanks for His infinite mercy and divine intervention.

In 1976, several things happened to me, and the choices that I made affect me today. In that year, I tried to kill myself. Then I left school three weeks before graduation. Then I left home before my dad returned from being sent somewhere by the air force.

I started going to a church in Fayetteville that seemed the very place I had been seeking for as long as I could remember. It was a place where I could get closer to God, walk in His presence, find His will, and please Him. I was also accepted by Him and others, and I was part of a loving family. Given that I was only eighteen years old, I felt good. God chose me as a son of God, and the pastor at this church could help me stay on the narrow path by revealing God's perfect will to me with every decision that came my way when I chose to take them to her, which I had to admit was not every time one came up. Maybe that is why I was told more than once that I was rebellious. Sometimes out of God's perfect will, I was brought back into line. For that above all was what I wanted: to stay in God's will and please Him.

In this same year, I was told that it was God's perfect will for me to marry Willie Clyde Norton, a man I did not know who was seventeen years older than me. At first I said no, and then I was informed that it was God's perfect will for me to marry him, and that if I did not, I would be falling right into the devil's plans for me. Satan wanted me to not be in God's perfect will.

Two months later, four days after I had turned nineteen, I was married to a stranger who came down to Fayetteville from Jasper, Tennessee, one week before we got married. At first I was told that I would have to take care of things because my husband was not able to. Then later I was told I was wrong for trying to be in control, when I had been in control of the finances and bill paying and such for years. I did not learn to trust Him as the head of the household; I had not learned to trust him as a man. I do love him and care for him, but not in the way a courted woman loves her mate whom she has chosen.

After twenty-three years of marriage, God brought us out of that church we were both a member of, and since then I have found out it was a cult with much control and fear abounding. Many battles later, my commitment is strong to stay married and see what God will do. He is working, but the past tries to hang on and drag me down as I try to shake it off. Please pray for us, and please do not pity us. In the name of Jesus Christ, there are no regrets.

Your sister in Christ,
Sheryl Sherry Lynn Norton

No Regrets
May 2002

The darkness tries to envelop me,
but the Light floods my soul.
Fingers of the past try to draw me back,
but love breaks their hold.
The pain of what might have been rears its ugly head,
But God's voice whispering, "Trust me," helps me to be bold.

In Jesus's name, there are no regrets,
for God is in control.
In Jesus's name, there are no regrets,
for in Him I am soundly sold.

God took me out of darkness and into His marvelous light.
He broke the chains that bound me tight and unlocked the prison door.
He kept me with His love, and He bound the wounds within my soul.

In Jesus's name, there are no regrets,
for God is in control.
In Jesus's name, there are no regrets,
for in Him I am soundly sold.

But things rose from the past that I thought were gone for good.
They tried to drag me down again, but only in God have I withstood.
For Jesus Christ, the Lamb of God, took away my sins.
He brought me out of darkness and made me whole in Him.

In Jesus's name, there are no regrets,
for God is in control.
In Jesus's name, there are no regrets,
for in Him I am soundly sold. Amen

Day 29: 1 Thessalonians 5:11–15

Day 30: Romans 12:3, 9–10

Month 5, Week 1

I received a phone call this morning. My best girlfriend wanted to share some words from a book she was reading. At times they were hard to hear, and at other times they helped a lot because I knew that I needed them. I am thankful that she even thinks of me, because her own plate is quite full. I have been so blessed to have known her and her family since 1976. We have been in and out of each other's lives since that time, but now we have an even stronger bond of friendship because we are more like family. It is nice being part of a family, especially with one where there is love. For the most part, there is love, and after what has transpired in the past, it is only by the hand of God and through His divine intervention that it is so. God is so good to us, though we do not deserve it. I thank God for His grace, mercy, and love.

A Friend, a Brother, a Lord
October 2000

A friend sticketh closer than a brother.
A friend goeth one more then due.
A friend giveth something for nothing.
A friend is Jesus Christ and a lot more for you and me;
He is the door.

A brother cares enough to say, "Whoa."
A brother picks you up when you fall.
A brother keeps you in prayer.
A brother is Jesus Christ, who laid down His life for thee,
that in Him there is hope galore.

A Lord knows who is His.
A Lord keeps His hand in the mist.
A Lord protects both day and night.
The Lord is Jesus Christ, who won the right after winning the fight. Amen.

Day 1: Proverbs 17:9, 13, 17

Day 2: Proverbs 18:8–9, 17, 19, 24

Day 3: Proverbs 27:6, 9–10, 17

Day 4: Luke 5:18–20

Day 5: Luke 15:6, 9, 21–24

Day 6: Job 19:13–14, 19, 21

Day 7: John 15:13–15, 17

Month 5, Week 2

Have you ever heard of getting married on a shoestring? Well, I did. The man I was to marry came down one week, and a week later we got married without any preparation. I did not have a nice white wedding gown, my hair was not fixed, I did not have nice shoes, and there was no ring or bridal bouquet. We exchanged Bibles, which were supplied by the man for whom I worked. The same day we got our wedding license, we got married. My parents were not there, and I cried.

Our marriage started out with less than two hundred dollars. We shared the apartment with the sister I stayed with before I got married, and the day after my wedding, I had to go to work. Neither one of us had much of anything to set up house with besides our clothes. We had three or four homemade quilts that my new husband had brought from home, plus our exchanged Bibles and our wedding license. That was about it.

One would not think that we would have made it with all that against us, but here we are after twenty-five years, soon to celebrate our twenty-sixth wedding anniversary through the divine intervention of God Almighty. though it has not always been easy. I believe that God protected us and honored the fact that we thought we were doing God's will and took a mate we would not have chosen for ourselves.

The Bride
June 2000

As I awoke, I kneeled and prayed
on what had been seen.
There was a bridegroom in all His splendor,
waiting for His bride.
His countenance glowed with anticipation,
waiting His bride to be.
The music started playing, and everyone turned to glimpse the bride.
What stood there waiting to come up the aisle was far from what she should be.
Her dress was wrinkled and full of spots,
and the hem was uneven with little tears all around.
Her shoes were very run down at the heels
and stained with muck and mire;
one strap held on by a pin,
the other one flapping loose.
Her veil had rends and wrinkles all around,
with hair that hung down limply, stringy, and dirty besides.
She carried flowers, faded and crushed,
and a Bible with its pages missing.

With row after row of pearls,
diamonds, emeralds, rubies, sapphires,
and gold weighing her down.

No, no, no, no!
Please do not present yourself to the bridegroom this way.
He deserves the best there is to give.
He has given the very best to us.
Can't you do the same?

So remake a new wedding dress,
no spots or stains at all.
The lacy trim so nice and smooth,
and clean about it there,
so neatly in its place front and back and sides.
The veil, crisp, white, and smooth,
on ringlets like a crown.
The flowers held in her hands,
so brilliant in color and lovely to behold.
The Bible was covered in calf's skin and gold upon its leaves,
every page accounted for, read, and believed.
The shoes of white with golden heels
and buckles on each strap—
they fit so well and looked so good on her dainty feet.
With one single strand of pearls and gold around her slender neck,
and a pearl and gold ring to put upon her finger.

Yes, yes, yes, yes!
This is more like He deserves,
the best that we can offer,
but this one and not the first.
Our time is drawing nigh, and the bridegroom is waiting for His bride. Amen.

Day 8: Matthew 22:2–4, 8–14

Day 9: Hebrews 13:4

Day 10: Revelations 19:7–9

Day 11: Isaiah 62:5

Day 12: Revelations 21:2–3, 9

Day 13: Matthew 9:15

Day 14: Matthew 25:1, 5–10

Month 5, Week 3

To be fair, I have to say my husband has been a good man and has been faithful to me in his commitment to our marriage. He has not been the kind of man who says "I love you" very much, and most of the time the only way I would hear it is if I say it first. Then he would tell me that he loved me also, but that did not happen every time either. The most important thing about him to me is that he is committed to following after God, as I am. He may have not been the husband I would have chosen for myself, but I have been blessed to be joined to a man of God who truly loves God. And even better, both are joined to the Bridegroom who is waiting for His bride.

The Bridegroom
May 2002

"My love," He whispers as the breeze through the trees,
and rumbles as the thunder in a storm.
My love watches over me as a soldier guards a palace gate,
protecting as a mother for her newborn.
The Bridegroom is my love for whom I speak,
and the one whom I adore.
The Bridegroom is my love for whom I speak,
and the one whom I look for.
My love, He called me unto Himself,
and told me of His great love that surrounds.
My love, He brought me out of the darkness
and broke off the chains that bound.
The Bridegroom is my love of whom I speak
and shall be forever more.
The Bridegroom is my love of whom I speak
and is the King, the Word, the way, as well as the door.
My love is He who had to leave
and promised to come again.
My love is called the Prince of Peace
and Savior of all men from sin.
The Bridegroom is my love of whom I speak
and has proved His love to me.
The Bridegroom is my love of whom I speak,
when He set this captive free in victory. Amen.

Day 15: Ruth 1:9

Day 16: 1 Samuel 1:8

Day 17: Isaiah 54:5

Day 18: Jeremiah 31:32

Day 19: 1 Corinthians 7:2–4, 10–11

Day 20: Ephesians 5:22–28, 33

Day 21: Titus 1:6–7

Month 5, Week 4

Have you ever wanted someone to love you so much that you would be willing to do anything for that person, even to the extent that you would lose your identity in the process? Have you found someone who loves you so much that He laid down his life for you? One who gladly took your place to keep you from a worse fate? One who, despite what you have done, loved you enough to draw you unto Himself, willing to forgive, willing to heal the wounds and adopt you into His family? One who has nothing but good for you, and who would be a friend, a provider, a guider through this world's jungle, a fighter for you? One who would even trade your death without Him for life with Himself, and a Father who will not leave you or forsake you? Well, there is such a one. His name is Jesus Christ, our Lord and Savior, and he's the Redeemer and our shepherd and elder brother.

Love Hung Himself upon a Tree
September 2003

Love came down to earth as man.
Love only did His Father's plan.
Jesus is our love;
Jesus is our life.
So come unto He who hung on high.

Love hung Himself upon a tree,
Taking the place of you and me.
Jesus is our love;
Jesus is our life.
So come unto He who hung on high.

Love took our place, dying for our sins.
Love rose again to bring us life in Him.
Jesus is our love;
Jesus is our life.
So come unto He who sits on high. Amen.

Day 22: John 1:16–18

Day 23: John 20:14–31

Day 24: 1 Corinthians 1

Day 25: 1 Corinthians 8:6

Day 26: 2 Corinthians 8:7–9

Day 27: Philippians 2:5–11

Day 28: 1 Timothy 2:5–6

Month 5, Week 5

God Almighty is our Creator, and unless we take the time to get to know him, we will continue to believe the lies that Father God's enemy would like you and me to believe about Him. Believe me, I am so glad I took the time for God's love. It's nothing like what man calls love; words fail to explain. A person has to experience God's love for himself or herself to know what I mean. The simple fact is that God is love, so experience God for yourself.

The Father of Father's Words
April 2001

I call you servants,
I call you sons,
and I call you kings and priests on high.

I call you precious,
I call you my children,
and I call you the apple of my eye.

I call you righteous,
I call you holy,
and I call you the anointed of God.

I call you conqueror,
I call you victorious,
and I call you the abundantly blessed ones.

I call you my body,
I call you the church,
and I call you the sheep of my fold.

I call you my lights,
I call you my written Apostles,
and I call you my vessels of gold. Amen.

Day 29: Deuteronomy 7:9–11

Day 30: Deuteronomy 30:5–10, 15–20

Day 31: Romans 5:1–21

Month 6, Week 1

Give God a chance to show you how much He loves you. He has nothing but good for you, if you give Him the opportunity to show you. The thing is that He will not force Himself on anybody. We have to want Him and call out to His Son to be our Savior because no man can come unto the Father except through His Son, Jesus Christ. We must ask Him to forgive us for all we have done wrong, and find out ourselves about God's love and awesomeness.

Love
December 2001

Love is the key to open locked hearts.
Love binds up wounds of those we have not had a part.
Love opens the doors and welcomes us in.
Love looks not upon the color of our skin.
Love knows no bounds when God lives in men.
Love gives much more than it receives.
Love caused our Savior to die on the tree,
Taking the place of you and me.
Love picks us up whenever we fall.
Love comes running as soon as we call.
Love forgives sin and gives us a fresh start.
Love puts back together a broken heart.
Love is kindness as well as good.
Love says, "I knew you could not,
But in God I could."
Love builds up what hate tears down.
Love draws a smile out of a frown.
Love says, "Let's use this, not waste it on the shelf."
Love thinks of others above oneself.
The love of God is real and true.
Won't you let Him love you too? Amen.

Day 1: Romans 8:31–39

Day 2: Ephesians 2:4–10, 14–22

Day 3: 1 John 4:8–16

Day 4: 1 John 3:1, 14–17

Day 5: Deuteronomy 7:6–13

Day 6: Ezekiel 16:8–14

Day 7: Proverbs 15:9

WAYS DIRECTED

Month 6, Week 2

"Which way do I go? Do I do this, or do I do that? How do I know I am making the right choice?" God's word is instruction to those who have chosen to follow after Him, and there are going to be plenty of choices along the way, whether or not we like it. Even if we choose not to follow after God, we have made a choice. Everything we do or don't, everywhere we go or not, we make choices.

Which Path?
August 2000

We all are on a path,
walking toward a goal;
Some are ahead, some are behind,
and some are walking beside us,
though we may not even know.

This path is rough, here and there;
it is also smooth without cares.

There are wildernesses, deserts, valleys,
and mountaintops high.
There are roadblocks, pitfalls,
and snares that try to snare.
There are detours, side roads,
and shortcuts galore.

It is our decision to follow Christ
or be driven tossed to and fro.
It is our decision to lay down our own lives
and pick up the cross to follow Him.
Let's eat, drink, and be merry, for tomorrow we may die,
then spend eternity in hell.

So on which path do you walk?
The slight path or the right path?
The old path or the bold path?
The spare all or the narrow path?
The laid-back path or the take-it-back path?
And last but not least,
the me path or the free path?

We are all on a path, walking toward a goal;
Some are ahead, some are behind,
and some are walking by our side,
though we may not even know. Amen.

Day 8: Psalm 119:5

Day 9: Deuteronomy 32:10

Day 10: Isaiah 8:11, 16

Day 11: Isaiah 40:14, 21–24, 28

Day 12: Jeremiah 6:8, 10, 18–19

Day 13: Jeremiah 31:19

Day 14: Philippians 4:11–12

Month 6, Week 3

Have you ever said, thought, or heard someone else say, "I think I can do it by myself." I have said it, and I found out I was wrong. It's like babies who have learned to walk. They want to step out on their own without help, only to fall on their cushioned bottoms. Well, I fell too, but I also found out that I could not do it alone. My Father God was there to pick me up, and now I hold tightly to His hand with every step that I take. Sometimes when I do not think I can take that step, Father God is there, encouraging me, reassuring me that He is right there through His word, and that I will not completely fail with His help.

God the Path Maker
May 2000

You set my feet on this path;
narrow is the way.
You set my feet on this path,
and here I am to stay.
You set my feet on this path
from darkness into light.
You set my feet on this path
from death into life.
You set my feet on this path;
hope is all around.
You set my feet on this path;
grace and peace abound.
You set my feet on this path
and saved my soul from sin.
You set my feet on this path,
and your blood cleansed all stains from deep within.
You set my feet on this path;
rooted and grounded am I.
You set my feet on this path,
I lift Christ Jesus high. Amen.

Day 15: Deuteronomy 4:31–40

Day 16: Deuteronomy 31:6–8

Day 17: Psalm 27:9

Day 18: Joshua 1:5, 9

Day 19: 1 Samuel 12:22

Day 20: Psalm 94:14

Day 21: Isaiah 42:16

Month 6, Week 4

In this life, I have to admit there have been a couple of times that I thought I was taking a step in the right direction or thought I knew the direction Father God was directing me, and I stepped away from His plan for this life that He has given me through His Son, my Lord and Savior Jesus Christ, only to have Him draw me back before disaster struck. I could have chosen to refuse to take heed of His voice, stamping off and muttering, "I know what I am doing. His way is taking too long. I do not feel right not being in control." Thank God that I did not do that often, and I hope I never will again. For in my weakness am I made strong in Him. God is my strength, and only through Him am I able; only in Him am I set free.

My Chosen Path
May 1999

I walked down the path till it became two.
I chose the narrow path, for it drew few.

Step by step I go on this narrow path;
step by step I go, looking not back.

This path isn't easy, but neither is it hard.
My Lord and Savior carried me when I got tired.

Day by day I go with Jesus at my side.
Day by day I go; His word is my guide.

Sometimes I rest along the way,
sometimes I run the race,
and sometimes I look into a glass and darkly see His face.

Foot by foot, the day is done;
foot by foot, the race is run.

The light, it shines upon my path;
darkness then is driven back,
and He bids me eat and drink my fill,
and know that Jesus Christ is real.
Piece by piece, I am sealed;
piece by piece, He is revealed.

He makes me king and priest on high.
Chosen son of God am I,
pressing on toward the mark to my crown, robe, and harp.

Line by line, His love is shown.
Line by line, God's Son is known. Amen.

Day 22: 2 Samuel 22:2–3, 7, 17–20, 30–35, 40

Day 23: Psalm 18:29–35, 39, 48

Day 24: Habakkuk 3:1–19

Day 25: Psalm 5:8, 11–12

Day 26: Hebrews 12:13

Day 27: 1 Corinthians 10:8–14, 23–26

Day 28: Jeremiah 18:1–11

Month 6, Week 5

How important are words to you? To me, they are a matter of life or death, light or darkness, love or hatred, joy or grief, hope or despair, good or evil. Words can either birth dreams or kill them. Words can either spring forth with life, hope, and purpose, or they can become shriveled up and dried out, lacking direction Words can either cause you to laugh with joy or cause you to cry in despair. This is why words are so important and valuable to me, and why the tongue, with help, should be tamed. It is such a small member but is full of poison. I am reminded of a scripture that says, "For out of the abundance of the heart the mouth speaketh, what a weapon it can be." So even to myself, I plead to be quick to hear, slow to speak, and slow to anger, as we are instructed by our loving Lord and Savior, Jesus Christ, the Word. Do not tear down with our words, but build up with our words in following God's Word and His Son, Jesus Christ.

The Word
June 2002

The Word is all-powerful.
The Word gives us life.
The Word illuminates every step we take.
For in the beginning was the Word,
and the Word was with God.
The Word was God, and the Word took on flesh and dwelled among us.
This is the Word that gives us hope, reveals His love,
brings us new life, and helps us find His way.
Therefore choose to speak the Word,
which builds up and restores a brethren to his faith.
Yes, words can be powerful with whatever we choose to say.
Yes, words can choose to heal and bring life,
or wound and bring death.
Yes, words they can illuminate with light as the day,
or be dark with the darkness of night.
The Word is all-powerful.
The Word gives us life.
The Word illuminates every step we take.
For in the beginning was the Word,
and the Word was with God.
The Word was God, and the Word took on flesh and dwelled among us.
This is the Word that gives us hope, reveals His love,
brings us new life, and helps us find His way.
Therefore choose to speak the words that bring life
and restore man to his proper place with our Creator, God Almighty,
our awesome God Most High. Amen.

Day 29: Genesis 45:12–13

Day 30: Deuteronomy 18:15–22

WHO IS HE?

Month 7, Week 1

Who is He? Who is Jesus Christ, God's Son? These are legitimate questions, and there are answers found in the Holy Bible, God's Word, in Jesus Christ. "For in the beginning was The Word, The Word was with God, The Word was God ... The Word took on flesh and dwelled among us ..." But how do we know unless we ask?

A Man's Question Answered
January 2000

There was a man who stopped and asked this question of me.
"How do you know there is a God, and where is He?"
All I could do was look at him, and then my answer came from within.

Do you see those trees?
Do you hear those birds?
Do you feel that breeze upon your skin?

Have you seen the mountains capped with snow?
Have you seen the valleys down below?
Have you seen the flowers grow?

Did you see that bird on the wing?
Did you see the stars gleam?
Did you see the flowing stream?

How about that rainbow after the rain?
How about that bear in the cane?
How about nothing being the same?

Yes, there is a living God, and He is everywhere we look.
Open your heart and receive His love, and ye shall not be forsook. Amen.

Day 1: Isaiah 9:6–7

Day 2: Daniel 3:24–25, 28–29

Day 3: Matthew 8:1–34

Day 4: Matthew 16:13–17, 20, 27–28

Day 5: Matthew 26:63–64

Day 6: Matthew 27:54

Day 7: Mark 1:1–2, 24–25

Month 7, Week 2

While this man called Jesus, the Son of God, was down here on earth, just what did He do? Well, if we were to write down everything that He did while He was here on earth, it would take so many books that we would not have enough time to read them all before we came to the end of our lives. Here is just a sample of what He did while here on this earth. You can find more things that He did in God's Holy Bible.

What Did Jesus Do?
July 2000

We wear leather on our wrists that says, "What Would Jesus Do?"
Well, why not ask,
"What did Jesus do for you and me?"
He healed the brokenhearted.
He made the blind to see.
He made the lame to walk again.
He set the captives free.
He turned the water into wine.
He calmed the troubled seas.
He spoke this world into existence.
His words caused devils to flee.
He walked upon water.
He healed a withered hand.
He straightened a woman's back
and tried to share His Father's plan.
Jesus said, "I do nothing that I do not see my Father do."
So He came to this earth as man
To live, learn, be obedient,
and prepare to die as God's sacrificial Lamb,
coming forth resurrected on the third day in victory,
but not to stay.
This is not even half of what Jesus did before He ascended in the clouds,
back up to heaven,
to sit on the right hand of His Father.
To God be the glory. Amen.

Day 8: Luke 4:18–19, 40–44

Day 9: Luke 12:4–9

Day 10: John 5:17–30

Day 11: Romans 8

Day 12: 1 John 3:1–8

Day 13: Matthew 8

Day 14: Matthew 12

Month 7, Week 3

God the Son is Jesus Christ. For God the Father, God the Son, and God The Holy Spirit are three in one. There is only one God, but three manifestations of that one God. Here is an attempt to describe God the Son, though there are many more facets to God than what I have set down here in this next poem.

God the Son
February 2000

With eyes like flames of fire,
a sword coming out of His mouth,
a golden girdle around His pap's,
and feet as fine brass.

A countenance brighter than the sun,
with hair as white wool;
riding a white horse,
ruling with a rod of iron.

He is the same today, yesterday, and forever,
the alpha and omega,
the first and the last,
the beginning and the end.

He is the Lord of the harvest,
the head of the Church,
the great I Am,
and the Bridegroom waiting for His bride.

He walks among the seven lamp stands
and holds the seven stars in His hand
that broke the seven seals
and judges man.

Who bears us about in His body and holds us in His hands?
Who sits on the right hand of His Father
and waits for the finished plan?

With a voice that sounds like thunder
and a whisper on the wind,
or many, many waters,
or a trumpet blast.

A roaring lion
or a meek lamb;
a gentle dove
or true God and true man. Amen.

Day 15: Isaiah 9:6–7

Day 16: Matthew 4:1–11

Day 17: Matthew 16:16

Day 18: Matthew 27:54

Day 19: Mark 15:39

Day 20: Luke 1:31–35

Day 21: Luke 4:32–41

Month 7, Week 4

Have you often wondered whether anybody was there watching? Was there anybody there to see what you were doing or to see what others are doing to you? Yes, God's eyes are everywhere at one time, and they don't miss a thing. They see the evil as well as the good, and they see what goes on in the light or in the dark. No one can hide anything from God.

His Eyes
June 2002

His eye is as a flame of fire.
His eyes are looking to and fro.
His eye is on the sparrow,
in the heavenly, or on the earth down below.
His eye is guiding the steps of a righteous man.
His eyes never close in sleep.
His eye sees all everywhere,
and from Him nothing can we keep.

Open the eyes of my heart
to see and understand Your will and Your ways.
Open the eyes of my heart,
and let me see them as You see them each and every day.
Open the eyes of my heart,
and show me all the tricks and traps that the enemy has laid.
Open the eyes of my heart,
and help me never to forget the price my Lord and Savior for me has paid.

Day 22: Genesis 6:1–8

Day 23: 2 Samuel 15:25–26

Day 24: 2 Samuel 22:28

Day 25: 1 Kings 8:29, 52

Day 26: 1 Kings 9:3

Day 27: 1 Kings 11:33–38

Day 28: 2 Kings 10:30–31

Month 7, Week 5

He was true God and true man, our Lord and Savior Jesus Christ. Through flesh He learned what it meant to be rejected, to be ridiculed, to be abused, to be lied about, to be falsely accused, to be with a home, to be without a place to lay His head, to be loved, to be taken care of, to count for something, and to be counted as nothing, among other things.

The Man
February 2001

Long, long ago and far away,
there was a man who died one day
upon a cross on a hill,
shedding His blood and making God real.
The man who died upon that cross was God's own Son
who came to save the lost.
He died to set the captives free,
but that's not all He did for you and me.
On the third day, He rose again,
conquering sin, death, hell, and the grave for all men.
He took our place who knew no sin;
His precious blood washes us deep within.
Jesus was the bridge between man and God,
to bring grace, mercy, and peace for soul's sake,
from God who sent Him who fulfilled the law.
Jesus was the bridge between man and God,
to bring Grace, mercy and peace for soul's sake,
from God who sent Him who fulfilled the law.
He left promising to return again,
to gather the wheat from the harvest into His barns.
King Jesus will rule with a rod of iron in His hand,
setting up His kingdom for His thousand-year reign on this land.
There is no end to this story from long, long ago.
Watch and see it unfold pure as gold. Amen.

Day 29: Mathew 22:16

Day 30: Mark 12:14–17

Day 31: Revelation 3:1, 7, 14

Month 8, Week 1

It is hard to imagine what it was like to be nailed to a wooden cross on a hill outside the city gates. It's hard to imagine the crowds of people cheering, laughing, and ridiculing. They seemed to enjoy watching Him suffer and were eager to see Him die. It's hard to imagine Him looking down from that wooden cross and seeing soldiers gambling over His garments. It's hard to imagine that on either side of Him were men who had done things worthy of their death, but not Him. "The Lamb of God, who takes away the sins of the world," "for He was wounded for our transgressions, He was bruised for our iniquity, and the chastisement of our peace was upon Him, and by His stripes we were healed." I do not think that we will ever be able to imagine what it was like to go through all our Lord and Savior, Jesus Christ, went through—and still he came out of it all victoriously.

Outside the City Gates
April 2001

Going outside the city gates
and looking upon that hill,
there were three crosses in a row,
and all of them were filled.

The first and third men on their crosses
were worthy of their deaths.
But the man on the middle cross was different from the rest.
The man who hung upon the second cross was innocent of all He bore.
They cruelly nailed His hands and feet
and did a lot more.

They scourged Him, mocked Him,
plucked out His beard, and stripped Him—and what for?
He was the precious Lamb of God
whose blood was shed for you and me.
He was the precious Lamb of God
whose blood washed away our sins and set us free.

The first and third man on their crosses,
their legs they broke to die quicker.
But Jesus Christ, the Lamb of God,
gave up His spirit; there was neither flicker nor sigh.
Going outside the city gates, looking upon that hill,
were three crosses standing in a row,
and all of them were filled.

On the first and third crosses,
on that hill were men guilty of all they had done.
But on that second cross hung God's own Son,
who paid the debt for all of man.
When He said, "It is finished,"
in Him we all won in death from sin,
and in life victoriously.
Guess what? It was all in the plan. Amen.

Day 1: Matthew 27:26–31, 35–38

Day 2: Luke 22:63–71

Day 3: Luke 23:20–26

Day 4: Mark 15:28–32

Day 5: John 19:23–30

Day 6: Acts 4:10–12

Day 7: Galatians 2:20–21

Month 8, Week 2

Do not take someone or something for granted. The only way to not take someone or something for granted is to appreciate that someone or something while you can. Do not take for granted that things can change, because what was not appreciated is seriously missed when it is no longer there. For example, one's health, seeing beauty, one's hearing, a sound mind, and a sound body, to name just a few. There are so many things that have not been added, like life, breath, love, joy, peace, dreams, hope, family, and children. The list can go on and on, but you can always add more. What I am getting at is that we tend to take for granted what has always been there, until we no longer have it. Let us not take God for granted, or the things that He has done, is doing, and will do.

Lord, You Didn't Have to Do It!
March 2000

At of the deep void of dark,
You spoke the light and spoke this world into existence.
Lord, You did not have to do it,
but I am glad that You did!

From the dust and the dirt and Your holy breath,
You fashioned man in Your own image.
Lord, You did not have to do it,
but I am glad that You did!

Even when man fell in sin and became Your enemy,
You bore with him and made another way.
Lord, You did not have to do it,
but I am glad that You did!

You loved us so much that You gave Your only begotten Son.
Lord, You did not have to do it,
but I am glad that You did!

And Jesus loved us so much
that He was willing to hang on the cross, shedding His blood,
to die and rise again in victory.
Lord, You didn't have to do it,
but I am glad,
oh, so very glad that You did! Amen.

Day 8: James 1:5–8

Day 9: Matthew 10:40–42

Day 10: Matthew 27:1–10

Day 11: Luke 12:1–9

Day 12: Psalm 100

Day 13: Romans 1:16–18

Day 14: Colossians 3

Am I the only one to wonder what these sayings and others like them mean? "You can't judge a book by its cover." "still waters run deep." "Looks can be deceiving." Well, through the years, I have had an idea. For many years, I was on the other side of the magnifying glass, being torn apart, belittled, and made the butt end of jokes for someone else's amusement. I have also been on the other side at times, until I realized what was going on. Have you ever let someone's like or dislike of another person color your opinion of that person without knowing the person for yourself? I will admit that there have been times when I have done that very thing, though now that I am a follower after Jesus Christ, with God's help I am made more aware of the old man's ways and the traps and snares of the devil. U have been given a way of escaping those temptations: through God, and by not sitting on God's judgment throne when He is the one and only true, righteous judge of all man, not me. We don't have to like what a person is doing, but that is not the person; it's what is in the heart that God sees, for what a man does is not who he is.

God, let us see them as You see them, and let us learn to love them as You love them. Help me to love the unlovely, for I have been one of those unlovely persons in my time, and I should not judge them. Amen.

Seeing Past
August 2002

A book's cover is not what's inside.
A turtle's shell only protects what it hides.
What you see may not be what you get,
for all that glitters is not gold.
See the unseen,
know the unknown,
and look through God's eyes, now being newborn.

A man puts on a mask to hide his face.
We use a shield to hide the vital place.
What we see is not what we get.
All that glitters is not gold.
Half a truth does not make it whole.
God. let us see things through Your eyes,
and not keep believing the devils lies. Amen.

Day 15: Leviticus 19:11–18

Day 16: Isaiah 11:1–4

Day 17: Matthew 7:1–2

Day 18: Luke 6:37–38

Day 19: Luke 19:22–27

Day 20: John 5:22–30

Day 21: John 7:24

Month 8, Week 4

God loves you—not what you do or have done but *you*! Even better than that, He likes you. You are not an accident or a mistake; you did not just happen. There is a reason why you are here, and you have a purpose and a mission. The only way to find that out is to turn to the one who created you and let Him show you. You are so very special to God. How can I say that? Well, think about it: "God so loved you that He sent His only begotten Son, that who so ever believed in Him would not parish, but have ever-lasting life" (John 3:16).

You, Yes, You
August 2002

You are special,
one of a kind.
There is no one else like you in the present or past.

You are loved
oh so very much.
Stop listening to the devil's lies.

You are liked by Me, so true.
For I gave My only begotten Son for you.

You are special
to My heart. Draw close to Me.
I've already done My part.
Love your Heavenly Father. Amen.

Day 22: Micah 3:11

Day 23: Matthew 7

Day 24: Luke 6:20–38

Day 25: John 5:17–47

Day 26: John 7:16–31

Day 27: John 8:12–35

Day 28: John 12:44–50

Month 8, Week 5

After I became a child of God, I started reading His word. The Bible tells us that we are precious in His sight, we are His beloved, we are the apple of His Eye, we are beautiful, we are made in the image of God, we are His treasure, we are the head and not the tail, we are above only and not beneath, we are sheep of His fold, we are wild olive branches grafted in, we are kings and priests, we are sons of God, and we are joint heirs with Jesus Christ.

This Family
December 2001

I was adopted into this family
I am proud to call my own.
A sister to all my Father's children, young and old forever more.
I was adopted into this family whose head is love personified.
I was adopted into this family where love and life reside.
I was adopted into this family, a king and priest on high.
Daughter of the great I Am Almighty, God Most High.
I was adopted into this family when my Father's Son became my Lord.
I was adopted into this family; I'll praise and rejoice in Him forever more.
Jesus Christ is my Father's only begotten Son.
Elder brother, king, and priest,
Lord and Savior, and a lot more.
"Why?" you ask. "How can this be?
Adopted by a Father you cannot see."
Oh, I can, and yes, I do in so many different ways.
He is in the light and beauty and heart-filled love of all I can survey.
His touch is warm; His arms are strong.
His love knows no bounds.
He proved that when He gave His Son,
who died upon a cross shedding His blood for you and me.
For it was He who took our place and bore our sins who loves us all, you see.
Open your heart and receive the love of the Father through His Son.
Be ye blessed and set free, choosing the Father's love and life.
Harkin to the Father's call and what the Son has done for all.
Let Him adopt you into this family;
you are precious in His sight.
He calls you His beloved child and the apple of His eye,
so let Him adopt you into His family and walk with Him always by your side. Amen.

Day 29: Isaiah 13:12

Day 30: Psalm 17:8

Day 31: Romans 11:16–18

Month 9, Week 1

God is a healer. At least, He is my healer, my great physician, my God who heals. He has brought me through a place where I found myself drowning in lungs full of fluid. I went into the hospital New Year's Eve, and thanks be to God, with prayers and the efforts of doctors and nurses, I came out February 7. There were about two weeks where I was not even aware of my surroundings, let alone what was being done on my behalf, in finding out what brought me to the hospital in the first place. During that time and since, I truly found out that God kept me, upheld me, and was with me, ever faithful.

Jehovah Rafa
July 2003

The God who heals is my healer too,
for by His stripes ye were healed.
See? It's already been done.

For it is God who heals the brokenhearted.
He makes the blind to see,
He makes the lame to walk again,
and He sets the captives free.
God is my great physician with healing in His wings.

He is my more-than-enough God
who has kept and upheld me in my need.

For it is God who heals the brokenhearted.
He makes the blind to see,
He makes the lame to walk again,
and He sets the captives free.

Turn to the God who loves you so,
and who can heal your every wound.
Turn to the one and only living God,
and see that His Word is true.

For it is God that heals the brokenhearted.
He makes the blind to see,
He makes the lame to walk again,
and He sets the captives free in victory. Amen.

Day 1: Genesis 20:17–18

Day 2: Isaiah 53:4–5

Day 3: Jeremiah 17:14

Day 4: Matthew 4:23–24

Day 5: Matthew 8:7–8, 13, 15–17

Day 6: Mark 1:30–34, 40–42

Day 7: Matthew 15:22–28, 30–31

Month 9, Week 2

I also mentioned prayer. I believe that the prayers of my husband and my church family reached the ears of God and prompted His divine intervention, releasing Him to intervene on my behalf. God is true to His word. He watches over His word to perform it so that it will not come back void. Prayers for others and oneself are vital in withstanding the attacks of the enemy, in walking successfully the path God has placed us on, and in running the race that is set before us. In my weakness, I was made strong in Him.

It's Prayer
August 2004

It's prayer that changes things.
It's prayer that makes the way.
Find His promises
And speak them out every single day.

It's prayer that changes things.
It's prayer that releases Gods hand.
Get in God's Word
And follow God's will and way for man.

It's prayer that changes things.
It's prayer that brings help on the run.
So kneel and pray,
And know that in God, we have won. Amen.

Day 8: 2 Samuel 7:18–29

Day 9: 1 Kings 8:22–62

Day 10: 2 Kings 20:2–5

Day 11: 2 Chronicles 30:27

Day 12: Nehemiah 1:4–11

Day 13: John 17

Day 14: Psalm 4:1–8

Month 9, Week 3

I appreciate the care that the doctors and nurses took of me, and I say God bless them. They are special people gifted with the desire to comfort and heal. I know there are some who are in it for the money, but there are those who really care and want to make a difference for someone who is suffering physically, and they desire to extend a helping hand, a comforting hand, a reassuring hand, a healing hand.

Hands
February 2000

Hands holding hands, strengthening the bonds.
Hands healing, anointed by God.
Hands helping man, pulling us out of the fire.
Hands reaching down, pulling us up out of the mire.
Hands gentle and soft,
for all those God has called and loves.
Hands hard in judgment,
for all those who have chosen nothing from above.
Jesus's hands are stretched out wide;
He bids us come and meet His bride. Amen.

Day 15: Genesis 5:29

Day 16: Deuteronomy 1:25, 27

Day 17: Deuteronomy 16:10, 15

Day 18: Deuteronomy 24:19–21

Day 19: Deuteronomy 33:11

Day 20: 2 Samuel 22:21, 35

Day 21: 2 Chronicles 15:7

Month 9, Week 4

Who is God? Who is God to you? To me, God is my Creator and the One who gave me life in Him eternally. He is my everything, my all and all. I did not know Him like I do now, and I still do not know Him as well as I would like, but I am still learning about Him. God is holy and righteous, and He is loving and kind. He is the one who upholds and keeps me, and He is my Abba Father and my Lord God Almighty. God is awesome and beautiful. I have not even begun to share with you who God is to me. I know from His word, the Bible, that He would like to be all these things to you and a lot more.

Stop limiting God. Stop putting Him in a little box that is only taken out when you need something from Him, or only on Sundays, and the rest of the week you live as it pleases you, ignoring Him altogether. God will not force us; we have choices. He is at the door of your heart, knocking. Choose to answer His knock. Allow Him to come in and be your Lord of everything. If He is not Lord of everything, He is not Lord at all.

God Is Greater Than All
October 1999

God is greater than all, and we should put our trust in Him.
Man is weak and tends to fall, and without Him,
we can do nothing of ourselves.

God is greater than all, and we should totally rely on Him.
Man sometimes fails to see others' needs,
but God sees all
and is mindful of those who come to Him and believe.

God is greater than all, and we should totally lean on Him.
Man, by leaning on his own understanding, faints.
But for those who lean on God,
He will never leave nor forsake.
God is our strength. Amen.

Day 22: Genesis 5:1–2

Day 23: Genesis 21:1–2, 12, 17

Day 24: Genesis 41:16, 25, 28, 32

Day 25: Genesis 49:24–26

Day 26: Genesis 50:19–20, 25

Day 27: Exodus 3:4, 6–7, 11–16

Day 28: Exodus 15:2–3

WHERE ARE WE GOING?

Month 9, Week 5

We, like the sheep, know the Shepherd's voice and go where we are directed. If we follow the Shepherd, who is our Lord and Savior Jesus Christ, the Son of God, He will lead us past the pitfalls, the traps, and the snares. Regardless as to what is going on around us, He will bring us through victoriously. If we choose to stray from the path He sets us upon, He will seek us out and try to draw us back to safety.

God the Path Maker
May 2000

You set my feet on this path;
narrow is the way.
You set my feet on this path,
and here I am to stay.
You set my feet on this path
from darkness into light.
You set my feet on this path
from death into life.
You set my feet on this path;
hope is all around.
You set my feet on this path;
grace and peace abound.
You set my feet on this path
and saved my soul from sin.
You set my feet on this path,
and your blood cleansed all stains from deep within.
You set my feet on this path;
rooted and grounded am I.
You set my feet on this path,
I lift Christ Jesus high. Amen.

Day 29: John 10:1–5, 7–8, 11–16, 26–29

Day 30: Ezekiel 34

Month 10, Week 1

This earth is not our home; we are simply passing through. We are strangers here, wanderers waiting to come home. For those of us who choose to make Lord Jesus our Savior and Redeemer, our home is in heaven. Everyone else will make their abodes in hell until they are cast into the lake of fire after the white throne judgment. There are no other choices; it will be in one place or the other.

A Wanderer Wandering
February 2000

A wanderer wandering through a land;
a stranger in this place.
A wanderer wandering through this land,
not knowing what there was to face.

From wilderness to valley,
from desert to mountaintop high,
from miry road to rocky road,
from wet road to dry.

A wanderer wandering in a land,
with Jesus as my guide.
A wanderer wandering in this land;
His love keeps me alive. Amen.

Day 1: Proverbs 12

Day 2: Psalm 16:11

Day 3: Proverbs 4:11–12, 14–15, 18–19, 25–27

Day 4: Matthew 7:13–14

Day 5: John 10:1, 7–10, 28–29

Day 6: 2 Peter 2

Day 7: Jude 1

HE IS

Month 10, Week 2

There is one of two places that we will be going. Before I truly came to God and accepted Jesus Christ as my Lord and Savior, I had a lot of fear and did not want to die. The questions were there, and I did not have the answers for them. Questions like, "What will happen to me after I die? Will it hurt? Will I be more alone than I am now? Is there anything more after death, or is that it?" I know now that for a follower of Christ, death of this mortal body brings one into the beginning of eternal life with God. As Christians, we do have a purpose here on earth, until it is time to go and be with God. What we do down here is just a shadow of what we will be doing in heaven. For those who choose not to follow after the one and only true, living God, it is clear as to where they will be, and that is hell—at least until the white throne judgment. Then they will be spending eternity in the lake of fire. God's word is clear on that.

The Portrait Gallery
November 2000

This gallery of portraits hanging on the wall
is a portrayal of life with man's victorious ascent
or downward fall with or without God.
The first is a portrait of a Shepherd watching carefully after His sheep.
This second one portrays a wolf among the sheep scattered to and fro.
The third portrays a beggar wounded, neglected, and sore at the gate.
Now, this fourth one you see is Jesus at the well,
the Living Water for you and me.
Looking on the fifth one, we see Jesus nailed to the tree,
giving His life's blood to cleans us from all sin setting us free.
In the sixth portrait hanging, there is a serpent under feet,
in which our Lord and Savior took from him the keys.
The seventh portrait hanging on the wall is a black, black open maw;
follow after Jesus, and in there you won't fall.
The last, portraying man's life, is two paths,
one narrow and the other wide.
The narrow path is straight away, and few walk there on.

The wide path is trodden down with way too many feet to count.
At the end of the narrow path is a bridge to heaven's gates.
Jesus is the only way to get to heaven's crown.
For those who chose the wide path, its end is hell alone.
Choose the straight and narrow way, and find peace untold.
Become a soul brought from darkness into the marvelous light,
and see God's love unfold to thee more precious than gold. Amen.

Day 8: Matthew 25:21, 23, 29–46

Day 9: Mark 10:14–15, 23–26, 30–31

Day 10: John 6:53–58

Day 11: John 12:23–26

Day 12: Romans 5

Day 13: 1 John 3:14–15

Day 14: 1 John 5:10–13

Month 10, Week 3

Think of it: our lives are like ships, and without the light source that can penetrate this present darkness, we will crash upon the rocks. Jesus is the light, and He can bring us into His safe harbor, keeping us from wrecking our ships, our lives. He is our source, a beacon in the time of trouble. When the storms of life are trying to overthrow us, Jesus is there, saying, "Peace. Be still."

Our Source and Our Light
July 2003

I saw the ship upon the sea.
It was a ship of flesh like me.

It went along its merry way
With no thought of the day.

Suddenly came this terrible storm
Bashing against this fleshly form.

When all seemed stark,
There was a light breaking through the dark.

Battered and bruised, limping in toward this safe harbor,
With its hull damaged so it's nothing like when it first started.
Arms reached out, bringing her in through the furious storm,
Cradled gently from the waves and the wind that tore at my form.

Now I know that Jesus is our source and our light,
Penetrating this present darkness.
Protecting us from those storms of life
That have tried to overthrow us. Amen.

Day 15: 1 Kings 11:36

Day 16: 2 Kings 8:19

Day 17: Psalm 27:1

Day 18: Psalm 119:105, 130

Day 19: Isaiah 9:2

Day 20: Proverbs 18:10

Day 21: Proverbs 29:13, 25–26

Month 10, Week 4

The Lord Jesus Christ is our Shepherd, and we are His sheep. He leads us beside the still waters and has us lie down in sheltered, comfortable places after we dine on the best, most tender, greenest grasses. We also get to feed on the choicest corn in the field. He takes care of His flock, keeping the bears, wolves, and lions away as long as we choose to stay under His protection. If we stray away, choosing not to take heed to His voice, all kinds of things can happen to us. There is an enemy, the devil, who would like to destroy us.

Are You the Shepherd's Sheep?
February 2001

Come to the well that never runs dry,
never runs dry,
never runs dry.
Come to the well that never runs dry, and never thirst again.

Feed in the pasture lush and green,
lush and green,
lush and green.
Feed in the pasture lush and green with what God sets before you.

Hear the Shepherd call His sheep,
call His sheep,
call His sheep.
Hear the Shepherd call His sheep and bring them into the fold.

See Him count them one by one,
one by one,
one by one.
See Him count them one by one to see that none are lost.

He leaves the ninety-nine to go after the one,
to go after the one,
to go after the one.
He leaves the ninety-nine to go after the one and hunts for it high and low.

"Hallelujah, I found my sheep,
I found my sheep,
I found my sheep.
Hallelujah, I found my sheep." He rejoices all the way home. Amen.

Day 22: Psalm 95:7

Day 23: Psalm 100:3

Day 24: Ezekiel 34:11–12

Day 25: Matthew 25:32–33

Day 26: Mark 6:34

Day 27: John 10:2–4, 11, 14–16

Day 28: Hebrews 13:20

Month 10, Week 5

When Jesus chose to take our place, allowing them to crucify Him, the Bible says, "He was like a lamb being led to the slaughter." Jesus was the sacrificial Lamb who takes away the sins of the world, and with the shedding of His blood, He cleanses us.

Are You Washed in the Blood of the Lamb?
August 2003

Are you washed in the blood of the Lamb?
Are you washed in the blood of the Lamb?
Are you chosen by God?
Are you cleansed and set free?
Are you washed in the blood of the Lamb?

There is power in the blood of the Lamb.
There is power in the blood of the Lamb.
Are you chosen by God?
Are you cleansed and set free?

There is power in the blood of the Lamb.
We are washed in the blood of the Lamb.
We are washed in the blood of the Lamb.
We are chosen by God.
We are cleansed and set free.
We are washed in the blood of the Lamb.

Thank You for the blood of the Lamb.
Thank You for the blood of the Lamb.
We are chosen by God.
We are cleansed and set free.
Thank You for the blood of the Lamb.
We are chosen by God.
We are cleansed and set free.
We thank You for the blood of the Lamb. Amen.

Day 29: John 1:29–36

Day 30: Acts 8:32

Day 31: Revelation 5:5–6, 8, 12–13

Month 11, Week 1

While standing on the beach and looking for the sun to rise, I was blessed to see the true sun of righteousness rising, more glorious than the creation. He appeared risen above the waves, with His hands stretched out toward we who were there on the beach, worshiping Him. I shared this moment to give you hope that God is with us and does disclose Himself from time to time. He is standing by, waiting for us to look for Him and seek after Him. When we do, we have been promised that we will find Him, because He is not a far off.

I Am Here
October 2002

I hear you calling Me; I am here.
I hear you crying out to be safe; come and draw near.
I am your God, and there is no other beside Me; look unto Me and be saved.

I hear you calling Me; I am here.
I hear you crying out to Me. Peace be still; do not fear.
If I be lifted up, I will draw all men unto Me; he who comes
unto Me, I will in no wise leave nor forsake.

I hear you calling Me; I am here.
I hear you crying out to be free from sin, death, hell, and the grave.
Just believe in Me, for he who has faith the size of a grain of a mustard seed, for him it will be.
So believe in Me as your Lord, and be free indeed. Amen.

Day 1: Psalm 9:9–10

Day 2: Psalm 34:7–10

Day 3: Psalm 40:16–17

Day 4: Psalm 69:32–33

Day 5: Proverbs 8:17

Day 6: Isaiah 11:10

Day 7: Matthew 6:32–33

Month 11, Week 2

My Father God is not a child abuser. He does not sit up there on His throne and laugh at us when we are going through hurtful and hard times. He does not have a magnifying glass, attempting to study His creations as they fall, fail, and struggle, only to parish while down here on earth. He is not busy elsewhere when we need Him. We should not blame Him for our choices or the choices of others.

Meet My Father
June 2001

Come let me introduce you to my Father
and tell you something about Him.

My Father is generous in His giving and is holy in all His ways,
and He is merciful from day to day to day.

My Father is creative and artistic,
and He is righteous and true.

My Father sits upon His throne in a place not made by hands.
He knows all about you and I,
and every step we take.

My Father is the husbandman; His Son is the true vine.
And He calls us, woos us,
and draws us to Himself through His Son, Jesus Christ.

My Father is God Almighty;
the one and only God is He.
He heals the brokenhearted;
He makes the blind to see.
He makes the lame to walk again,
and He sets the captives free.
My Father is God on high,
who also lives within me.
He is my fortress, my shield and buckler,
and my safe hiding place from the enemy.

My Father is the great I Am
who loved so much that He gave.
He won the battle over sin, death, hell, and the grave
when He came and took our place. Amen.

Day 8: Deuteronomy 30:19–20

Day 9: Joshua 24:15–22

Day 10: Job 34:4

Day 11: Proverbs 1:25–30

Day 12: Proverbs 3:31–35

Day 13: Isaiah 7:15–16

Day 14: Isaiah 66:4

Month 11, Week 3

Who are we? Whose are we? As much as we might think so, we are not our own persons. We belong to either God or to the devil. We walk in either the light or in the dark. We choose either life eternal with Him, or death without Him. There is no other choice, as much as we might have been told differently.

Which Are We?
May 2000

The Bible asks these questions of man.
Which do you choose?
Good or evil,
light or dark,
full of wisdom or foolish in your ways?
Are you a worm or a butterfly,
sheep or goat,
a flock of sparrows or an eagle flying high in the sky?
Are you wheat or terres,
earthly or heavenly,
baring all your burdens or casting them on Lord Jesus this day to stay?
Are you tossed and driven or peace being still,
truth or lie?
Is your hope in Christ, or are you denying Him and accepting a lie from the wrong guy?
Jesus is the only way.
He stands at the door—will you give Him His say?
He died so that all would be set free.

His blood was shed, and it cleansed me.
When He died, He rose again.
Now we are all set free who come to Him. Amen.

Day 15: Ecclesiastes 12:13–14

Day 16: Deuteronomy 30:15–20

Day 17: Joshua 24:14–15

Day 18: Proverbs 1:23–29

Day 19: Philippians 1:22, 27–30

Day 20: Matthew 7:12–14

Day 21: Matthew 25:46

Month 11, Week 4

Jesus Christ, God the Father's Son, came down to this earth, took on flesh, and dwelled among us. That is what the Holy Bible tells us, and so Jesus does know all about pain and suffering. When He was thirty-three years old, He went to Jerusalem, taking upon Himself all our sins. He bore in His body all our sickness and diseases while hanging upon that old, rugged cross on that hill called Calvary. He was given thirty-nine stripes across His back before being nailed to that cross. The Word tells us that He was wounded for our transgressions and was bruised for our iniquity. The chastisement of our peace was upon Him, and by His stripes we were healed. He became sin who knew no sin. Right before He died, He spoke and said, "It is finished." All that needed to be paid was paid in full at that time. Then He was taken down from that cross and placed in a borrowed tomb. On the third day, He rose from that tomb, and after a time He ascended on high, in the clouds. That's not all. He is coming back!

Paid in Full
April 2000

The loveliest rose that I have ever seen is a blood-red rose
that reminded me of the blood that was shed
while He was nailed to the tree.

"What's that?" you say.
"Who was He that was nailed to the tree?"
He was the Lamb of God who did no sin,
wrongfully accused and His Father's only begotten son.

The lion of Judah, who sits upon His throne.
Emanuel whose love He did show. The Messiah whose battle was not with man,
but the prince of darkness of this land.
His only crime was His love for man
and following His Father's plan.

For this, they nailed Him to the tree.
Drop by drop, His blood was shed,
washing away our sins.
All that kept us away from God
was placed upon Him then.

Then they took Him off the tree,
when life had fled away.
They placed Him in a borrowed tomb
until the third day.

That's when the rock was rolled away, and God said, "Come forth, My Son."
Jesus won the battle over death;
He is the victorious one.
Yes, the debt has been paid in full,
for all those who come unto Him.
Yes, the debt has been paid in full,
when He said "It is finished!" Amen.

Day 22: Luke 1:31–33

Day 23: Luke 2:6–7

Day 24: Luke 3:6–7, 16–17, 21–22

Day 25: Luke 4:16–19, 40–44

Day 26: John 3:13–18

Day 27: John 19:1–6, 14–18

Day 28: Luke 24:1–12, 51–53

Month 11, Week 5

Yes, He is coming back. He will be setting up His kingdom for a thousand-year reign on this earth. At least, this is what the Word tells us. Maybe you're asking, "Is this true? Can I really believe these words?" Well, let me ask you: Can you afford not to believe them? How much are you willing to gamble on where you spend eternity? Has everything that has been written about Jesus Christ up to now come to pass? If you do not know the answers to these questions, as well as others, you might want to find out for yourself. God loves you. God is not running from you, so quit running from God and His truth.

Face What You Don't Like
May 1999

Strolling down the road of life,
not knowing what was in store,
I tried to build myself a wall,
not wanting to see anymore.
I tried to hide myself away;
I tried to keep the wolf at bay.
After many years, I awoke
knowing that my wall was broke.

Life has been marching by.
Wait for me; I want to cry.
All I know is I have to face
that I am in the human race.
Building walls and closing eyes
won't keep time from passing by. Amen.

Day 29: Revelation 11:15–18

Day 30: Revelation 20

Month 12, Week 1

Where is Jesus in this life that you have been given? Is He high and lifted up? Is He acknowledged at all? Are we following Him, or is He pursuing us? The Bible tells us Jesus Christ is seated on the right hand of the Father in heavenly places. Those who have chosen to make Him Lord are in Him, and He is in them. He did come down to this earth manifested in the flesh to take our place, but afterward He went back to His Father, and He is waiting to come again.

Who and Where Is
July 1999

Who is God?
Don't you know?
He is our Creator.
Who is Jesus?
Don't you know?
He is our Lord and Savior.
Who is the Holy Ghost?
Don't you know?
He is our comforter and friend.

Where is God?
Don't you know?
In the third heaven.
Where is Jesus?
Don't you know?
Seated on the right hand of His Father.
Where is the Holy Ghost?
Don't you know?
He is everywhere.
If ye are seeking, then ye shall find
answers to these questions.
If ye knock,
the door shall open to guidance and direction.

When we except Jesus Christ as Savior of our souls,
our Lord and God Almighty brings us into the fold.
In knowing the Father, you must know the Son,
and finally find His abiding love.
There is no price that we must pay;
God has already made the way. Amen.

Day 1: Ephesians 1:20–23

Day 2: Ephesians 2:5–10

Day 3: 1 Corinthians 1:21–31

Day 4: 2 Corinthians 13:4–6

Day 5: Ephesians 2:14–22

Day 6: 1 John 5:1–5, 10–13, 18–20

Day 7: John 15:1–8

Month 12, Week 2

We are seated together with Him in heavenly places. Who is "Him"? He is Christ Jesus, our hope. He's the alpha and omega, the beginning and the end, the first and the last. We, as God's children, are in Him, and He is in us. We are sons and daughters of God and are joint heirs with Jesus Christ; we are kings and priests on high. Jesus is the Lord of lords and King of kings, the Prince of Peace. He is in us, and we are in Him, seated in heavenly places. While we journey in this land, though it may seem that we are traveling alone, we are not alone. He is to be found if we simply seek Him. As a matter of fact, God is pursuing us.

Hope in Jesus
April 2000

You have drawn me out of darkness,
into the marvelous light,
now standing at the throne in the presents of my God,
falling at His feet like dead but yet alive.
Even in the darkness, there is light,
now sitting with Jesus at our Father's right.

There is hope in Jesus all along the way.
There is hope in Jesus, who turned night into day.
There is hope in Jesus, who shed His blood for me.
There is hope in Jesus, who set the captive free.

Light the darkened pathway with God's holy Word,
looking unto Jesus in death and rebirth.
The loving Shepherd, God's sacrificial Lamb
who bore all on His shoulders, is the great I Am.
So look up to the hills from whence comes our help.

Put your hope in Jesus all along the way.
Put your hope in Jesus, who turned night into day.
Put your hope in Jesus, who shed His blood for thee.
Put your hope in Jesus, who set the captive free.

Look upon our Lord nailed upon the tree.
He said, "If I be lifted up, I will draw all men unto Me."
Shedding His blood, He died, was buried, and rose again for you and me
to set all free who believe.
So my hope is in Jesus all along the way.
And my hope is in Jesus, who turned night into day.
And my hope is in Jesus, who shed His blood for me.
And my hope is in Jesus, who set this captive free. Amen.

Day 8: Hebrews 3:1–4, 6, 12–15

Day 9: Deuteronomy 10:14–15, 17, 20–21

Day 10: Psalm 136:1–7, 26

Day 11: Revelation 17:14, 17

Day 12: Isaiah 9:6

Day 13: Luke 24:19, 46

Day 14: Romans 9:28–29, 33

Month 12, Week 3

There is a song I learned that says, "I'm the resurrection, and the life. He that believeth in Me though he were dead, yet shall he live, yet shall he live, and who so ever liveth and believeth in Me, shall never, never die." When we accept Jesus Christ as our Lord and Savior, we are new creatures in Christ Jesus. This body may die, but the Spirit of God dwelling in us lives on, either with God or separated from God for eternity. Jesus died but yet lives. He is our pattern and example. The tomb was not His bed for very long.

Not for Long His Bed
March 2000

The foxes have holes, and the birds have nests,
but the Son of man hath no place to lay His head.
The fish have their schools, and the ballplayers have their teams,
and the Lamb of God was sacrificed alone for thee.
The rain has its rainbow, and the door its key,
and the Shepherd of the sheep was who died to set man free.
The rose has its thorns, and the oceans its seas,
while Jesus was who was nailed on a tree.
The fire has its flame, and the lettuce its head,
and Christ's tomb not for long was His bed. Amen.

Day 15: Matthew 25:46

Day 16: John 3:13–21

Day 17: Romans 5

Day 18: Romans 6

Day 19: 1 John 3:1–10, 14–15, 23–24

Day 20: 1 John 5:1, 5–6, 9–13

Day 21: Jude 1:7

Month 12, Week 4

Can you picture this? Jesus is teaching a group of men when another group comes in demanding that Jesus judge a woman who was caught in adultery, and they are ready to stone her. He then stoops down and begins writing in the dust. They ask for the third time what should be done with this woman who was found in adultery, trying to trap Him. He calmly says, "He without sin, cast the first stone." Men start dropping the stones they had been carrying, and one by one they leave without a word. The leave the woman with Jesus, who forgives her of her sins and sends her on her way with the words, "Go and sin no more." The Son of God, Jesus Christ, did what He saw His Father do in showing mercy, forgiveness, and love, because God is love.

Go and Sin No More
July 2000

With eyes downcast, weak with fear,
hopelessness and despair filled her mind.
Forced to stand in the midst of them
and this man they called Lord.

What has she done?
Why was she there?
Master, this woman was taken in adultery.
The men held stones in their hands,
waiting for the Master to speak
While He was writing something in the dust at their feet.

He spoke at last, saying these words to all the men there.
"He without sin may cast the first stone,"
was simply all He said.

One by one, they dropped their stones,
turned, and walked away.
Not one remained of those who came;
only He and the woman were left.

He paused His writing in the dust
and asked, "Woman, have you no accusers?"
With a voice filled with shame,
the woman said, "No, Lord, none remained."

With loved-filled eyes, He looked at her and said, "Neither do I.
Your sins have been forgiven you.
Go and sin no more."

With tear-filled eyes and a grateful heart,
she went away saying,
"Truly He is the Lord." Amen.

Day 22: John 8:3–11

Day 23: Romans 6:14–16

Day 24: Psalm 91

Day 25: John 5:14

Day 26: 2 Peter 2:20–22

Day 27: Matthew 9:2, 5–6, 12–13, 22, 29–30

Day 28: Mark 2:5, 9–11, 17

Month 12, Week 5

The time is short; the end is drawing near. The signs reveal that we are in the end-times. We need to be watching for Lord Jesus's return and keep ourselves occupied in God's work until He comes. The Bible also tells us that we are to love His appearing. Now, we still have a choice, but the time is soon coming when there will be no more time to choose. Then it will be too late. Please do not wait until there is no more chance to choose. Now is the time. Pray this prayer and believe in your heart, and you will be saved.

God, You said in Your Word that if I believe in my heart You raised Jesus from the dead and confess with my mouth to Jesus as Lord, I would be saved (Rom. 10:9–10). So I now confess, Jesus as Lord, and believe You raised Him from the dead for me. I thank You, Father, that Jesus is now my Lord. You are now my Father, and I am born again, saved. I now have a home in heaven. Jesus is my Lord. Thank You, Father in Jesus Name. Amen.

Now:

July 2004

Now is the time.
This is the day of salvation.
Let King Jesus be your Lord.
Let Him save you from an eternity without Him.
Make yourself ready, for He is on His way.
Maybe not today, maybe not tomorrow.
Maybe not next week, or maybe not even next year.
But why gamble with your eternity?

Don't look back; don't waste another minute.
There is no time to lose.
The enemy's lies have put you to sleep.
The enemy's lies have closed your eyes.
Wake up! Wake up! Wake up!
Shake yourself from the dust.

Be ye ready before His return.
Be ye ready before it's too late.
Let King Jesus find you about our Father's business.
Let Him find you watching for His return.
Now is the time.

This is the day of salvation.
Now is the time.
Go ahead and live—don't wait. Amen.

Day 29: Isaiah 45:18–23

Day 30: 2 Corinthians 6:2

Day 31: Mark 16:16

Extra Pages

Printed in the United States
By Bookmasters